SOAP M

Mac

Making Soap

The Ultimate Gui

Soap Making Made Easy: Making Soap from Scratch

The Ultimate Guide to Soap Making

By: Geraldine McDaniel

9781632874719

PUBLISHERS NOTES

Disclaimer – Speedy Publishing, LLC

This publication is intended to provide helpful and informative material. It is not intended to diagnose, treat, cure, or prevent any health problem or condition, nor is intended to replace the advice of a physician. No action should be taken solely on the contents of this book. Always consult your physician or qualified health-care professional on any matters regarding your health and before adopting any suggestions in this book or drawing inferences from it.

The author and publisher specifically disclaim all responsibility for any liability, loss or risk, personal or otherwise, which is incurred as a consequence, directly or indirectly, from the use or application of any contents of this book.

Any and all product names referenced within this book are the trademarks of their respective owners. None of these owners have sponsored, authorized, endorsed, or approved this book.

Always read all information provided by the manufacturers' product labels before using their products. The author and publisher are not responsible for claims made by manufacturers.

This book was originally printed before 2014. This is an adapted reprint by Speedy Publishing, LLC with newly updated content designed to help readers with much more accurate and timely information and data.

Speedy Publishing, LLC

40 E Main Street,

Newark

Delaware

19711

Contact Us: 1-888-248-4521

Website: http://www.speedypublishing.com

REPRINTED Paperback Edition: ISBN: 9781632874719

Manufactured in the United States of America

DEDICATION

This book is dedicated to my grandma Louise. She taught my mom how to make homemade soap and also taught her grandchildren. This process is something I will treasure as I got to spend a lot of time with her and I learned much more than how to make soap.

TABLE OF CONTENTS

Chapter 1- A Brief History Of Soap Making

The art of manufacturing soap has been, in a measure, known and followed for many ages, proving a source of industry and advantage to various nations and individuals. It may therefore interest some of our readers if we attempt to trace its origin and progress as indicated by the writings of the earlier authors.

Pliny, for instance, the Roman historian, informs us that the art of manufacturing soap is the invention of the Gauls, and that the best article made by them was a combination of goats' tallow and the ashes of the beech-tree. They also seem to have been acquainted with both hard and soft soaps.

The Romans eventually acquired this knowledge from the Gauls, by whom this branch of industry was, with their conquests, soon spread over Europe. Whoever may have been the originators of soap making, the Romans were undoubtedly familiar with it.

Galen, at least, mentions it in his works, and confirmatory of this statement, we may add that a soap maker's shop, with its utensils and products, was discovered among the ruins and ashes of Pompeii, which was destroyed by an eruption of Mount Vesuvius in the first century of the Christian era.

Soap was often used by the Romans as a cosmetic, for Pliny tells us that soap, with which the Germans colored their hair red, was imported into Rome for the use of the fashionable ladies and their gallants in that city. This cosmetic was probably tinged with the juice of a plant.

But before we recur further to less remote times, we will endeavor to answer the question, "What substitutes were employed previous to the invention of soap?"

Soap, both hard and soft, as it is well known, is produced by the union of the fats and the alkalis; by hard soap, we mean such as have soda, and by soft soap is understood that which has potassa for its basis. Water alone will not remove oily substances from any surfaces to which they may adhere, but a solution of soap, being always more or less alkaline, though its constituents may be united in their number of equivalents, will, nevertheless, render the oil freely miscible with water, so that it can be easily erased.

A similar effect is produced by using a mixture of water and lixivious salts. The gall of animals and the juice of certain plants, also possess the property of removing dust and dirt, It does not, however, appear that gall was employed by the ancients, but it is certain that in washing they used saponaceous plants.

In the remotest times, it appears that clothes were cleaned by being rubbed or stamped upon in water without the addition of any substance whatever. We are told by Homer, that Nausicaa and her attendants washed their garments by treading upon them in pits containing water. We find, however, at a later period, that mention is made of ashes and a lye of ashes, but it is so seldom noticed that their primary use cannot be ascertained.

Aristophanes and Plato mention a substance, "konia," which they say was employed for washing purposes, and Pollax leads us to infer that this " konia" was a lye of ashes. With this lye, oil and wine jars were cleansed, as well as the images of the gods.

The practice of de-carbonizing alkaline lyes by means of lime, was, according to Beckmann, known at any rate in the time of Paulus Aegineta, but we are not led to suppose that the Romans were acquainted with the dry substance obtained by evaporation of the clear liquid.

Various ancient writers inform us, furthermore, that lixivious natural salts were employed for washing, such as the nitrum, designated "borith" in the writings of the Hebrews. In the present day it has commonly been supposed equivalent to nitre, but this is an error, for it has been evidently proved that the ancients understood by the word nitrum, the carbonated alkali either of potassa or soda. Both of these substances are natural products, and found in many places and in large quantities, either in outcrops of different rocks or prairies, or in springs and lakes.

Asia is rich in such lakes; some exist in Asia Minor, Armenia, Persia, Hindostan, Thibet, and other eastern parts of that continent. Egypt, also, is richly supplied with soda lakes and springs, and with mineral sodas, whilst in Naples a volcano rock is still extant containing soda.

As some of these substances are highly impregnated with hygroscopic salts, it is not necessary to suppose, as some do, that the Egyptians produced their mineral alkali from the ashes of plants; on the contrary, Pliny states that they were obliged to put it-in well-corked vessels, otherwise it would become liquid.

The production of alkali from plants seems to have been the invention of a later period. Strabo speaks of an alkaline water in Armenia, which we have reason to believe is similar to that of the lake Ascanius mentioned by Aristotle, Anxigonus Carystrius, and Pliny. And here it is worthy of remark, that the ancients made ointments of those mineral alkalis and oil, but no hard soap.

The cheapest and most common article, however, used for washing was the urine of men and animals. This, not long since, was actually employed in the cloth manufactories at Leeds, Halifax, and other places in England. To obtain a supply of it, the ancients deposited at the corners of the streets, special vessels, which they emptied as soon as filled by the passers-by, who were at liberty, even expected, to use them.

Scourers at Rome, however, were obliged to reside either in the suburbs or in unfrequented streets, on account of the consequent disagreeable odor attending their business. Instead of soap, the ancients at any rate made use of the saponaceous juice of some plant, but of which one it is difficult, we may say impossible, to define.

Pliny speaks, among others, of a plant growing on a rocky soil and on the mountains, with prickly and rough leaves. Fuchs was of the opinion that it must have been the soap-wort, still used in Italy and

France. Others imagine that it was the Gypsophila Struthium, of Linne', a plant with a tender stem and leaves like those of the olive tree; but Beckmann places no confidence in any of these surmises, but rather favors the idea that it was a plant growing in Syria. Beanmeal was also employed for cleansing purposes.

Large quantities of fullers' earth (silicate of alumina), at the same time were moreover used, and clothes, dressed with this earth, were stamped upon by the feet, a process by which grease is partly absorbed and partly scoured off.

The poor at Rome, moreover, rubbed it over their clothes at festivals, in order that they might appear brighter. Some of these earths were employed in the baths instead of nitrum, and De la Valle, who traveled through the Levant at the beginning of the last century, states that the practice was still in vogue and adopted by persons of the highest distinction; they, in fact, never bathing without it.

It has, furthermore, been authentically established, that in the eighth century there were numerous soap factories in Italy and Spain, but it was not till the close of the twelfth and commencement of the thirteenth century that this branch of business was gradually introduced into France.

The first factories were founded in Marseilles, an old colony of the Phenicians, a race half Grecian, half Egyptian, energetic, intelligent, active, particularly partial to industrial arts and commercial enterprises. This ancient city was, as it were, the cradle of soap manufacturing.

Here all the crude materials for this purpose were abundant. The fecundity of its soil gave rise to the olive tree of the Orient, as well as to the vegetable sodas, whilst its harbor in the Mediterranean peculiarly favored and hastened the prosperity of the soap manufacturers and traders. There has, indeed, been gradually a considerable increase in the demand for soap, attributable mainly to the method of bleaching linen, first adopted in the seventeenth century, at which time this new branch of manufacture was imported from the West Indies, and the important application of the chlorine for bleaching textile fabrics had not been discovered.

Notwithstanding the richness of its soil, and its natural resources, Marseilles, nevertheless, could not furnish the crude materials in quantities sufficient to supply the wants of her soap manufacturers, and consequently, ere long, became tributary to Spain and Italy, to the former for the oils and vegetable sodas; to the latter for the oils only.

From France, the art of manufacturing soap was introduced into England at an unknown epoch prior to the year 1500. Soap, for a long time, was there made partly according to the French method, viz., with sodas obtained from the incineration of seashore plants, and partly after the German plan with potash and salt, which plan is still followed by some old-fashioned soap makers. Almost all kinds of soap were thus manufactured in England, whilst in France the olive oil soap only was produced.

About the first decennium of the present century, however, palm oil and cocoa oil soaps have been made in Paris, where also the art of manufacturing toilet soaps has scarcely been superseded by either English or American manufacturers.

The application of rosin for making soap is of English origin. When the art of soap making was introduced into this country, it is difficult to ascertain, but it is certain that the great impulse which the art received originated in 1804, from the genius of Le Blanc, by whom soda was economically extracted from common salt, and eventually introduced into the English market by Mr. James Muspratt, the owner of extensive chemical works.

This discovery, moreover, one of the most beautiful and important in modern chemistry, inaugurated a new era, as it were, in the art of soap making. Not less important were the investigations of Chevreul in 1811, by whom the proximate constituents of the fats, scarcely known before, were exactly demonstrated.

He, in fact, may justly be regarded as the savant who elevated this industrial branch from a mere trade to a prominent art, which at the present day is characterized by the introduction of new saponifiable substances from all parts of the world, by the application of ordinary and superheated steam, and by various mechanical arrangements for different processes of pressure; quite recently also, use of pressure has been made by which equally mild and detersive soaps are produced at a cheaper rate and less waste of time.

Composition of Soaps

Soaps are not, as is generally supposed, the result of the direct and integral union of fats with alkalis. The chemical action which produces saponification is of a very complex nature. The art of making soap dates from a very early period, and though it was known that certain fats heated with caustic lyes formed soap, still the theory of the union of oils and alkalis was not satisfactorily ascertained and established till the French chemist, Chevreul, about fifty years ago, unerringly proved---1st. That all fatty matters known as oils, butters, and suets (with very few exceptions), consisted partly of liquid and partly of solid ingredients, such as the stearine, the margarine, the oleine, the butyrine, etc.

2nd. That these ingredients, or proximate principles, are decomposed, by the action of alkalis, into their components, consisting of the sweet principle of fat known as glycerine, and certain fatty acids, called the stearic, margaric, oleic, acids, etc.

3d. That the solidity of mutton suet, of beef tallow, and hog's fat, is chiefly attributable to the stearine and margarine; and the liquidity of oils, to the oleine.

Upon this theory, it follows that when fats or oils are heated with caustic lyes, a combination of fatty acids with alkali is formed; this operation is designated saponification.

Several attempts have recently been made to substitute petroleum for fatty matters in the manufacture of soap, but had the theory of saponification been fully understood by such parties, they would not have wasted their time and money in so hopeless an enterprise.

Soaps are divided into hard and soft, the former having soda, and the latter potash for their bases. The former, however, is the most extensively manufactured, being universally in demand, whilst that for the latter is very limited, particularly in this country. Acids decompose soaps; combining with their base and expelling the fatty acids, for these latter being insoluble in the former, float on the surface of the liquid. By this means, consequently, soaps are easily analyzed, but on this subject a special chapter is devoted in the present work.

We have deemed it expedient thus briefly to introduce to the notice of the reader, the theory and principles on which saponification is based, for though practice alone can teach one how to make good soap, it is obviously expedient that he should be somewhat acquainted with the laws of chemical affinity, by means of which, those numerous phenomena occurring in the manufacture of soap may be more readily understood.

Chapter 2- Which Tools are Required To Make Soap

This chapter deals with cooking soaps, and mentions producing soaps in extremely large quantities. Smaller batches can also be made on your stovetop using stainless steel pots (nothing made of aluminum should ever be used).

Stainless steel pots for cooking and mixing, wooden spoons for stirring, and pyrex glass dishes for measuring and pre-mixing are safe and suitable for preparing your soaps. A Rubbermaid tea pitcher is strong enough to mix your lye and water.

Safety Note: Always wear rubber gloves and eye protection when preparing soaps, and NEVER use the same dishes that you mix or measure your lye or fragrances in for cooking or food.

Whether steam be employed or not, these are made of wood, or wrought-iron, or cast-iron, or bricks lined with glazed stone. Their dimensions necessarily vary from two hundred to four thousand gallons, according to the extent of the manufacture; but the larger the caldron, the better, as much labor, fuel, and lye are thus saved.

One hundred pounds of fat will require a thirty-five gallon caldron, and a ton of the same material will need a vessel of a capacity of about seven hundred gallons. The shape is invariably cylindrical, being widest at the top, having usually (indeed they ought always to have) a faucet for the purpose of discharging the spent lye.

Brick kettles, though costly, are best in one respect, viz., they retain heat the longest during the paste operation. The bottom of these, if desired, can be composed of brick when steam is employed, whilst in other cases, a metallic bottom is absolutely necessary. As, however, cracks at the juncture are occasionally caused by the unequal expansion of brick and metal, much caution should be exercised in the structure of such kettles.

The thickness of the walls also, should be regulated by the size, and the inside built with glazed stone, whilst the whole, exterior and interior, should be cemented with pozzuolan earth mixed with sand. To make them still safer, it would be judicious to hoop them with strong iron clamps.

Boiling Pan with a Wooden Curb

Cast-iron kettles are, for the most part, only found in small factories, for in larger establishments, merely the lower portion is made of cast-iron, and the upper of wood or brick.

In purchasing kettles manufactured entirely of cast-iron, the thinnest should be selected, which are always composed of finer and denser grain, and can be more easily filed than the thicker.

In every instance, too, the soft iron is preferable to the brittle, being more durable; but with regard to durability, it should be borne in mind that sheet-iron kettles will last longer than the cast-iron.

They, also, when burnt through, can be satisfactorily repaired, whereas the others are altogether useless, and new ones have to be supplied.

Here, again, the soft sheet-iron (and that of the first quality) should be selected, the bottom piece being from three-eighths to one-half an inch in thickness, and the sides from three-sixteenths to one fourth, according to the dimensions. Much attention should also be paid to riveting the pieces so that no aperture is left. The rivets in the lower third, moreover, should be inserted evenly with the bottom (countersunk), otherwise the workman cannot go smoothly and thoroughly over it with his crutch, a necessary process to prevent the soap from burning.

Heating the Pans with Open Fire

Common kettles, which are to be heated with open fire, should be so constructed that the heat may circulate at the bottom before it enters the chimney. In kettles, however, designed for soap-boiling, the heat must be confined to the bottom, for if it be allowed to circulate around the sides, the ingredients would inevitably be burnt.

In order thus to circumscribe and condense the heat, it is necessary that

1st. The grate is placed in the center of the hearth and vertically below the kettle.

2nd. The inside of the fireplace be built of refractory bricks, in order that the heat may be thrown back below the bottom of the kettle.

3rd. The fuel employed be that which produces the most heat and the least flame. Hence hard coal should be selected.

4th. The openings through which the products of combustion enter the chimney, possess together the same surface as the grate; experience having shown that this is the best method for obtaining a good draft and effecting a complete combustion of the fuel.

The sides are composed of brickwork, erected and lined with cement (mortar resisting the action of water). The upper part, which never comes in contact with the fire, and is intended to afford space for the soap to rise, expands in the form of a cone.

The fireplace B is separated from the ash-pit H by the grate r. The fire, after having heated the bottom of the pan, passes by the flue located half round the side of the pan into the chimney A. This is accessible for the purpose of cleaning by the door x; the soot is thrown into the pit .

A tube, with a cock, leads from the lowest part of the pan for the removal of the under lye. The whole of the pan is sunk into the floor of the boiling-house, which is made of planks, stone, or iron-plate, in such a manner that the brickwork of the upper part projects to about three feet above the floor.

Heating Pans with Steam

Both ordinary and superheated steam (i. e., of a temperature over 212), are employed for the above purpose; but the latter is far preferable, because, as before stated, the heat can then be introduced directly into the material, whereas ordinary steam has to be condensed through a worm, or conveyed intermediately under a kettle with a double bottom, and a tube for the discharge of the condensed vapor.

A worm or such a kettle is requisite, otherwise the quantity of water condensed would be so voluminous, that hard and grain soaps could not be boiled to "strength."

By applying superheated steam, now almost universally adopted in chemical establishments, both time and fuel are saved, because such high-pressure steam mingling with the fat, increases the necessary agitation of all the ingredients, thus facilitating and expediting saponification.

These advantages not only accrue in large factories, but also in those where they boil perhaps merely twice per week. A steam-boiler, eight feet in length and three feet in diameter, with two atmospheres pressure, will easily manufacture weekly, 100 cwt. of soap.

Again, it should be remembered that much less fuel is consumed in generating steam to obtain a given amount of heat, than when it has to be produced by an open fire; in the former process, also, less watching is requisite, and several vessels can be boiled at the same time, though only one fireplace be used, whilst in the latter much heat is lost by the absorbing effect of the brickwork, and by its unavoidable escape through the chimney.

Among other advantages of steam, we may mention that not only can wooden vessels be used, but also that the temperature can be regulated and kept at a certain degree by simply turning the stopcocks; the fats combine more readily and rapidly with the alkalis; the boiling is uniform throughout the whole mass, and the soap never burns.

The manufacture may be carried on in a smaller building, and the vessels placed on any spot within the range of the steam-generator.

CHAPTER 3- ALL ABOUT LYE

There are some safety measures you should follow when working with lye, first and foremost you should always wear hand and eye protection, and when mixing your lye with your water you should ALWAYS pour your lye into the water, and not the water into the lye. Adding the water into the lye could cause a horrible and dangerous chemical reaction.

This alkali is called in commerce, vegetable alkali, sal tartar, pearlash, potash, and hydrated protoxide of potassium. When the crude potash has been subjected to the heat of a reverberatory furnace, the product is termed pearlash. In commerce, it is found in solid hard pieces, interspersed sometimes with bluish, but oftener with reddish spots; oxide of iron, and a trace of sulphide of potassium, being the cause of the latter discoloration.

The sal tartar is simply purified pearlash. Potash itself is derived from certain plants, and especially from forest trees. These are cut down, converted into ashes and lixiviated. The liquid thus obtained is evaporated until it is brought to a solid state. This residue is subjected to the heat of a reverberatory furnace, for the purpose of drying it completely and freeing it from its sulphur and organic particles. In this state it is offered and sold in the market as pearlash.

Plants and trees, however, are not the only sources from which it is derived, for it has recently been manufactured from certain crystalline rocks, from feldspar, for instance, which yields 17 percent. of oxide of potassium, and about 5 percent is said to be producible from the New Jersey and Delaware green-sand.*

According to the species of plants and trees from which they are extracted, and the soil upon which those plants and trees grow, potashes contain a larger or smaller amount of carbonate of potassa (exclusively valuable to the savonnier) as well as of other substances, such as sulphate of potassa, chloride of potassium, carbonate, phosphate, and silicate of lime, the two first only being soluble in water. In addition to the carbonate of potassa, the American potash contains for the most part, caustic potassa.

Ure found in the best pink Canadian potashes, almost uniformly, sixty percent of absolute potassa, and in the best pearlash fifty percent; the alkali of the former being nearly in a caustic state, but that of the latter carbonated.

Soda

Soda is of much more importance to the manufacturer of soap than potash, because he could not make the hard soap without it. It is found in a natural state on this continent, in Venezuela, and in Mexico, and when thus found it is called native soda.

Urao is the term by which it is known in Mexico and in South America. The amount of native soda is, however, gradually decreasing, and totally inadequate to supply the proportionally increasing demand. A small fraction only of this surplus is derivable from the incineration of certain sea and shore plants, and by far the largest portion now used is acquired from the transformation of salt.

The best quality of native soda, and most appreciated in this continent, is generally imported via England from Spain and the Levant, and known as barilla. It contains from fifteen to thirty percent of carbonate with a little sulphuret, and is mixed with sulphate and muriate of soda.

Spanish sodas are very extensively used in England, being considered superior to the artificial, inasmuch as the hard soap is thereby found to be less brittle and more plastic, a peculiarity which in Ure's opinion is attributable to the small proportion of potassa which they always contain.

Such sodas, moreover, and especially those extracted from plants, and possessing a considerable quantity of the chloride of sodium, were formerly exclusively used in the manufacture of the Marseilles olive oil soap during the salting operation, called by the French relargage.

It was also further used in the second and third boiling. In lieu, however, of this kind, the salted soda,-the "soude salee," —an artificial soda, is substituted in Marseilles, and is almost universally used at the present time; the method of manufacturing which, as has been previously remarked, is based upon the preparation of sulphate of soda from salt, its transformation into crude carbonate of soda (designated black ash), and the purification of the crude soda by lixiviation, evaporation, and calcination. The product thus obtained is termed white ash, or soda ash.

According to Morfit, the standard of good soda-ash in our market is 80 percent carbonated, calculated both from caustic and carbonated soda. Soda is found in commerce purer than potash, and mostly with uniform properties. Indeed, potash is often adulterated with it, owing to its cheapness.

Caustic Soda

It is only within the last few years that the caustic soda has been offered in, the market, and can be purchased either as a solid or a liquid. In the latter state, it is denominated concentrated lye, and soap makers find it a most convenient commodity, as it saves them the trouble of preparing it themselves.

It is well known that a certain weight of caustic soda represents a larger amount of soda combining with the fats than the ordinary soda. We found it always nearly caustic. Both red and white, of equal value, are in the market, but a prejudice exists against the former, the soap makers being impressed with the idea that it is not as well adapted for their business as the latter.

Their prejudices, however, are very groundless, for when the red caustic soda is dissolved, the coloring matter gradually settles at the bottom, and the liquid becomes entirely clear. In Europe they now use for making caustic soda, large quantities of a mineral called kryolithe, which is found in Greenland.

Bottled distilled water is preferred liquid used by modern soap makers, and no tests are needed to determine if it's suitable for making your soaps. Distilled water makes a nice lathering bar of soap.

Only spring or river water should be used in making soap, which, moreover, must be perfectly clear, otherwise clear lye cannot be produced. It must also be free from organic matters, for these are often dissolved, and though imperceptible, soon cause the water to become putrid.

Nearly all waters contain mineral matters in solution. Hard waters, for instance, contain a certain amount of carbonate of lime, gypsum, chloride of calcium, and magnesium. When such waters are used, though the lyes be equally good, and the process of saponification not impeded, still there will be a loss of material in proportion to the quantity of alkali neutralized.

A water containing more than twelve grains of such substances in one gallon, should be rejected. If hard water be used in soapboiling, the quality is not injuriously affected (as in dyeing), nor, we repeat, does it retard the process (as is the case in brewing, for such waters act against fermentation). But it is, for the above-mentioned reason, a good plan, to make a careful examination of a certain kind of water before using it. For such cases, the services of a chemist will be required.

Preparation of the Lyes

The following information is not something you'll need to know if you plan to use red devil lye, as this lye is already packaged and prepared properly.

Lye is an aqueous solution of caustic soda or potassa, and by the agency of which the chemical decomposition of the fat and its conversion to soap are effected.

Caustic soda, indeed, is at present a commercial commodity, but it may occasionally happen that the savonnier will. have to prepare his own lyes from the carbonates, especially the potassa. Hence the expediency, in our opinion, of describing the method by means of which lyes can be prepared. They can be prepared in two ways.

One plan is to reduce the soda or potassa into pieces about the size of a nut, mix it with slacked lime, let it stand twenty-four hours, and then leach it out with water.

For this purpose, they have in France tanks of brickwork or sheet-iron, capable of holding from two hundred to five hundred gallons, and having a perforated floor, placed from two to four inches above the bottom, and covered with a layer of straw, on which is poured the mixture of lime with the alkali.

A faucet is inserted between this perforated floor and the bottom, by means of which the liquor can be drawn off.

The lyes prepared in this way are called " lessives faites a froid," but these are never perfectly caustic; whilst in this process, though possibly the most convenient, more lime is requisite than when the following method is adopted, which results in the formation of perfectly caustic soda. The potash or soda (not too concentrated a solution), should be thoroughly brought together with lime-milk, this process being sustained with heat. The carbonic acid of the alkalis thus uniting with the lime, forms insoluble carbonate of lime, which settles at the bottom. We stated above, that the solution of the alkalis must not be too strong; it moreover must be of a definite concentration.

A French chemist, for instance, ascertained that it was necessary that there should not be more than fifteen percent of alkali in the solution; otherwise there would remain a portion of the carbonated alkali undecomposed.

Suppose one hundred pounds of pearlash have to be transformed into caustic potash; for this purpose, a one hundred and fifty gallon kettle, containing eighty-five gallons of water, should be heated with steam or open fire; and when it boils, the pearlash, having been previously pulverized, should be gradually dropped in, stirring it all the time.

As soon as it is thus dissolved, forty-eight pounds of slacked lime, made into milk of lime, should also be gradually put into this boiling liquor. Experience has proved, that for the thorough decomposition of the carbonates of the alkalis, the process of boiling must be continuous and uninterrupted, and the lime of a milky consistency, not in pieces, nor in powder.

In order to ascertain whether the lye is caustic or not, take a test-glass full, let it stand till cool, then filter, and drop into the clear liquid some nitric acid; if it effervesce, the lye is not caustic, and vice verse; when not caustic, the boiling has to be continued till the portion taken from the kettle shows, when filtered, no escape of carbonic acid, if nitric acid be added.

As soon as no carbonic acid escapes from the lye, thus tested, the fire should be taken out, the liquor carefully covered, and suffered to remain undisturbed for twelve or fifteen hours, so that the lime may settle.

After this, the clear liquor should be transferred by a siphon into a wooden vat, lined inside with sheet lead, and having a cullendered false bottom, and cock fitted near the bottom (see Fig. 5), so that the clear lye may be drawn off.

The number of vats necessary, depends, of course, on the amount of business transacted, each of which should be kept carefully covered.

The remainder in the kettle, containing yet some lye, may be lixiviated two or three times with water, for though weaker lyes are thereby thus obtained, they are nevertheless serviceable at times.

The lime used must be of a good quality, and not been exposed to the atmosphere. Fat lime is best; only the quantity actually required should be slacked at a time, because the hydrate of lime (as well as the lyes) loses its causticity when exposed to the air.

CHAPTER 4- THE PURPOSE OF SAPONABLE FATS

The following information is something every good soap maker should learn. Superior soaps can be made if you know the properties of oils used in soap making, as well as the benefits of using each respective oil.

Helpful Hints: 60% Olive Oil, 20% Coconut Oil and 20% Palm Oil makes an extremely nice hard super lathering bar of soap.

Also plain lard makes a nice batch of soap for low cost that many have found to clean clothing as well as skin extremely well. If you cannot obtain the more exotic oils, then plain lard (make sure the lard doesn't have a strong foul odor) makes a superior batch of soap. 4 oz. bars can be sold for $1.00 each, and you'd still make a tremendous profit.

To make a super silky batch of soap you can use, Cocoa Butter (25%), Coconut Oil (15%) Shea Butter (15%) and Olive Oil (45%). This makes a super hard bar that is tinted an off yellow color, that leaves skin feeling silky, smooth and refreshed after use. This batch would be quite expensive to make, but well worth the costs to any that enjoy using this recipe. I regularly sell my bars made using this recipe for as high as $5.00 per 6 oz. Bar.

All the naturally occurring fats are mixtures of substances, the constituents of which are similar to the salts which inorganic chemistry embodies, i. e., we find in the fats several organic acids and bases.

For instance, the sulphate of soda, or the glauber salt (in daily use) is the combination of an acid (the sulphuric acid) with a base (the soda). The fats are, similarly, combinations of acids (the fatty acids), with a base (the fat base).

The difference between the constitution of an inorganic salt (as above described), and those of fats, is simply this: in the former there is only one base with one acid, in the latter several fatty acids are united with one base, whilst others also have several bases.

The most common fat base is the oxide of glyceril (with which we are unacquainted in its pure state), but which we know unites with water immediately after its separation from the other constituents of the fats, and thus forms the glycerine, or sweet principle of oils.

In the salting operation, this glycerine sinks below the lye, and becomes dissolved in the brine.

The most common fatty acids are: the margaric, the stearic, and the oleic, which, uniting with the oxide of glyceril, form the margarine, the stearine, and the oleine, of which, in various proportions, all fats consist.

The margarine is found principally in the butters, and not drying vegetable oils, the stearine in the suets, and the olein constitutes the liquid portion of most animal and many vegetable fats; in these latter, too, palmitin, another principle, and somewhat resembling margarine, is sometimes traceable, especially in the palm oil.

The palm oil has also this additional peculiarity, that it contains free acids, the quantity of which increases with its age, and hence the reason why old palm oil saponifies better than fresh.

Pelouze and Boudet found in one sample of fresh palm oil, one-third free acid, in another, one and a half, and in a third, nearly four-fifths of its weight. There are, moreover, found in fats, tissues, albumen, traces of slime, pigments, and often peculiar acids, which impart to them a peculiar odor.

In regard to the mutton and goose fat, Chevreul has proved that they owe their strong and penetrating odor to a peculiar substance which he calls hircine.

Having thus made, as we think, some necessary remarks on the immediate principle and nature of the fats, we proceed to a special consideration of the various fats, and first we will speak of the vegetable fats or oils.

They have generally a very different consistency; some remain liquid at a temperature of +5 to +40 F., some, as the olive oil, solidify at the freezing-point of water, whilst others coagulate at a temperature of 50 to 60 F., as is the case with the palm oil and coconut oil; these are also called butters.

All the oils, with few exceptions, are lighter than water; their specific gravity oscillates between 0.919 and 0.9 of 0. They, however, have many properties in common, as, for instance, they are both liquid at a temperature of 65 to 85 F., and both insoluble in cold and hot water, but easily soluble in ether, and all of a sweet taste.

Exposed to the atmosphere for some time, many undergo remarkable changes. Some solidify, others thicken and become hard, but retain their brilliancy.

Vegetable oils have consequently been divided into two classes, into the drying or siccative, and into the fluid or non-siccative oils. Of the first named, are oil of linseed, hempseed, and poppy oil. Of the second, olive oil, palm oil, sweet almonds, and coconut oil. According to the mode of obtaining oils, we distinguish oils of the first and second pressure. Experience has shown that those of the second pressure are more serviceable to the soap manufacturer, for though less liquid and often mucilaginous, they nevertheless contain more stearine, and we must remember the richer the oils are in stearine, the harder are the soaps they yield.

Coconut Oil

This substance, also called coconut butter, is found in a liquid state in the nut of some palm species, growing in Brazil, Ceylon, and at the coasts of Malabar and Bengal. In commerce, the nut is called "copperah" it yields sixty percent of the fatty substance.

The cocoa butter is white, sweet, and of the consistency of lard, of a mild taste, and when fresh, of an agreeable odor. Its melting-point lies between 60 and 70 F., and it becomes easily rancid.

Six different fatty acids have been discovered in the cocoa butter, most of which being solids, accounts for the great firmness of the soaps it forms. This fat is also remarkable in another relation, uniting with soda lyes in any proportion, without separating from them.

Owing to this exceptional property, this fat is used in large quantities for the making of filled soaps. It is very slow to unite with lye by itself; it is therefore usually applied in combination with tallow or palm oil, increasing their emollient properties, and also giving to the tallow soaps a brilliant whiteness.

Palm Oil

This fat, which owing to its consistency, should more properly be called palm butter, is obtained from the fruit of several varieties of palm trees, growing especially in South America, at the western coast of Africa, and in the East Indies.

The Canary Islands and Madeira, also furnish us palm oil. The commercial oil never is identical in its composition, which difference probably must be ascribed to the state of maturity of the fruits, and especially to the varieties of the trees from which the oils are extracted.

The palm butter is of an orange color, and when not rancid, of a violet odor. The commercial kinds have different denominations; the prima lagos and secunda lagos are considered the best.

The melting-point of the fresh crude palm butter, is, according to Payen, at 80 F., while it is of a much higher fusing-point when old.

In commerce, we find sometimes a fictitious article, which is nothing more than tallow and lard melted together, colored with natural palm oil and aromatized with powdered orris root.

This article, however, is easily distinguished from the natural palm oil, for the genuine is soluble in acetic ether, whilst the spurious will not dissolve.

Palm oil is employed both in the bleached and in the natural state. In the bleached state it produces a soap of most beautiful whiteness, and rich with the characteristic odor of the oil, especially when the oil is operated upon by the chromic acid process, which we propose to describe hereafter.

For the bleaching of 1000 lbs. there is necessary 5 lbs. red chromate of potassa, 10 lbs. strong hydrochloric acid, and 2 ½ lbs. sulphuric acid.

First, the chromate of potassa is pulverized and solved in hot water (twenty pounds of water will be enough to effect solution). The palm oil should next be transferred in a wooden tank, and heated with steam until 120 F. are reached; this temperature obtained, the steam is turned off and a portion of the solution of the chromate of potassa is added, agitated, and a proportional portion of hydrochloric acid added; at last the sulphuric acid.

After thoroughly agitating this mixture with the oil for a few minutes, the oil changes in color, becoming first black, then dark green (of the resulting oxide of chromium), and soon afterwards light green, when a thick froth appears on the surface, which appearance is an indication of the completion of the process.

If a sample of the oil, when taken out and allowed to settle, does not appear sufficiently decolorized, an additional portion of the bichromate of potassa, with muriatic and sulphuric acids, should be added. The process is completed in from twenty to thirty minutes.

The whole has to be left quiet for one hour, so that the solution of the resulting salts may settle. The clear oil is then drawn off in a wooden cask, mixed with some water, and heated again by the introduction of steam. It is again left alone for some time, and the fat subsequently drawn off.

In making soaps palm oil is usually employed with tallow, in the proportion of twenty to thirty of the former to one hundred of the latter.

It is also usually employed in making rosin soap in order to correct the flavor of the rosin and brighten the color.

Olive Oil

Olive oil is procured from France, Spain, Portugal, Italy, Greece, Northern Africa, and from the islands of the Mediterranean. It seems to have been known from antiquity, for its mode of manufacture is mentioned in holy writ, and what is remarkable it has but little varied since.

We distinguish particularly three kinds of oils, namely: the oil of the first pressure, or virgin oil (huile fine on vierge) obtained by a gentle pressure of the freshly gathered fruit; a second kind is gained by submitting them, when thus pressed, to the action of hot water and pressing them between metallic plates previously heated; and the third inferior kind (called les ressences) is the product of this residuum, or marc, when boiled in water.

Only these two latter kinds serve in the manufacture of soaps; often they are adulterated with cheaper oils.

In the order of the affinity of the fatty bodies to the alkalis the olive oil occupies the first rank; it yields, also, a very excellent soap, highly estimated for its fresh and agreeable odor.

It is very extensively used by soap manufactories in Marseilles and for the well-known Windsor soap.

An old receipt prescribes nine parts of good ox tallow and one part of olive oil. There is very little demand for it in this country, probably owing to its costliness, and it is seldom used, except in the limited manufacture of the finest toilet soap.

Oil of Poppy

This name is given to the product, on pressure, of the bruised seed of the Papaver somniferus. It is whitish-yellow, inodorous, of an almond taste, and when pure less viscous than most oils, and remains liquid even to 0 F. It belongs to the class of drying oils.

Seeds of poppy are brought from the East Indies to some extent for oils. It is especially used for the manufacture of soft soaps; and in France it is employed with tallow for the manufacture of an imitation Marseilles soap.

Galam Butter

In addition to the above-described fats, we will mention three fatty bodies, of the consistency of tallow, which have lately been brought into the English market. The galam butter is the product of the Bassia blutyracea, a tree growing in Africa.

It is of a reddish white color, mild odor and taste, and saponifies readily. It has been found to contain eighty-two percent of stearine, and eighteen percent of oleine, and is solid at 85 F. Another fatty substance, met with in Africa very often by travelers, is obtained from the butter tree of Shea; it was discovered by Mungo Park.

Stillingia Butter

Stillingia butter is a fat exported from China, and obtained by pressure from the fruit of a tree growing in the valley of Chusan. It is of a brilliant whiteness, of little or no odor, harder than the common tallow, and fuses at 99 F.

As to the method of obtaining it, and from what part of the tree it is extracted, various and very opposite opinions are entertained.

Mafurra Tallow

Mafurra tallow is a newly-discovered fatty matter, extracted by hot water from the mafurra kernel; these kernels are of the size of a cocoa bean, which abound in Mozambique, Madagascar, and the Isle of Reunion.

It has a yellowish color, and an odor similar to that of cocoa butter. It is less fusible than tallow, and with the alkalis forms a brown soap. It contains a large percentage of solid fat, and it is said to be easily procurable at a cheap rate.

Animal Fats

Though identical in their elementary composition with vegetable fats, they are nevertheless distinguishable by their color, odor, and consistency, as well as by the larger proportion of-stearine and margarine they contain. It is to these constituents that the animal fats owe their solidity.

There is, however, also a great difference in the consistency of the animal fats, whilst the richer they are in solid constituents, the higher is their melting-point.

In the Cetacei, a class of whale fishes, the fats are generally fluid; in the carnivorous animals soft and rank flavored; and nearly scentless in the ruminants; usually white and copious in well-fed young animals; yellowish and more scanty in the old.

The degree of firmness, moreover, is not the same in all parts of the organism. The fat of the kidneys is generally harder and more compact than that found in the cellular tissues and in the bowels of animals.

In general, the fat of the female is softer than that of the male, easily perceptible, as the tallow of the ox compared with that of the cow.

Even the climate has its influences, for we find that in the temperate zone, the fats have greater hardness, and are more compact than those of colder countries; the same may be said of the seasons, as we find that the fat of animals killed during the summer months is much softer than that of animals killed during the winter.

The nourishment, also, has a marked and material influence; for the dryer, more substantial, colder the fodder, the better and harder will be the fat. Oil cakes and distillery slops diminish the consistency of it.

The color and odor of the fats have, of course, effect in the manufacture of soaps; but interesting and useful as these details are, we are obliged to abridge them, and pass to a more special consideration of the fats.

Beef Tallow

Of all animal fats, this is the most used. Its general characters are well known; it has a yellowish tint, due to a peculiar coloring matter, separable by several washings in hot water, and is firm, brittle, but not so white as mutton suet. That rendered by steam, as is now universally done in France, is generally the whitest.

The melting-point of beef tallow we found to be as high as 111 F., and it can be cooled down to 102 F. before it becomes solid again.

Among the varieties of tallow which appear in commerce, the North American is the most in demand (it contains about seventy percent of stearine). The Russian tallow is also much esteemed; less so the tallow from South America.

Mutton Suet

Mutton suet is generally compact, firm, whiter, and has less odor than beef tallow; however, when the fat is stale the smell is most disagreeable and nauseating.

Mutton fat, moreover, is richer in stearine than beef tallow, and is consequently much sought after by the tallow as well as the stearine candle manufacturers.

Saponified with soda lye it yields a beautiful white soap, but being so rich in stearine it is liable to become too hard and brittle. In order, therefore, to obtain a milder and more unctuous product it is generally mixed with fifteen to twenty percent of lard or coconut oil, whereby a superior soap is obtained, especially adapted as stock for the manufacture of toilet soaps.

Hog Fat (Lard)

This is generally prepared from the adipose matter of the omentumrn and mesentery of the hog, by freeing it from the membranous matter connected with it, washing with water and melting it with moderate heat, so as to separate the fat from the cracklings.

In this state it is an important article of trade. Western lard is generally rendered by steam; it has also a granular appearance, and can be pressed for oil without any further granulation.

Corn-fed lard has the most consistency, made-fed is next in quality, while that obtained from hogs, fed on distillery refuse, is thin, flabby, and deficient in body.

Lard has, when fresh, a mild and agreeable taste, the consistency of butter, and its melting-point is at 81 F. It consists of sixty-two percent liquid fat or oleine, and thirty-eight percent of solid fat.

When granulated and pressed at a low temperature, it yields a fluid, denominated lard oil, which, as a commercial commodity, varies materially in quality.

The pressed cake, consisting chiefly of stearine, is termed solar stearine, and exclusively used in the manufacture of candles.

Lard is an excellent material for soap manufacturers; it forms a white, sweet, and pure soap. For the purpose of rendering it more frothing it is saponified either with tallow or coconut oil.

Bone Fat

Bones contain, on an average, about five percent of fat, brownish-white in color, and of an oily consistency. Only fresh bones are adapted for the extraction of fat, because when bones are kept for some time, the fat permeates the texture of the bones in such a manner as to render its extraction very difficult.

Where no machinery is used, the bones are generally split up lengthways by a hatchet, boiled in water, by means of which the fat is evolved, decanted, and filtered.

For purifying and deodorizing bone fat, Mr. H. Schwarz recommends to melt the fat and a small quantity of saltpeter together, and afterwards add a sufficiency of sulphuric acid, to decompose the latter.

The mass scum's very much, becomes of a light yellow color, loses its noxious smell entirely, and furnishes a fat very well adapted for soaps.

Fish Oil

Fish oil is a term applied to various products very different in their origin.

The fat of several species of whales, for instance, is employed to obtain fish oil, such as the cachalot, the pot-fish, the whale of Greenland, the Antarctic whale (Balena Australis), different dolphin species, the narvall, the sea-porc, and several species of robben and mammifera belonging to the class of whales.

According to the origin, consequently, there are different kinds of fish oil in the market. The oil, for instance, which flows out spontaneously from the fat heaped up in a reservoir, is called white fish oil.

There are also boiled fish oils, and, under the name of train oil, a variety of inferior qualities are included. For their further purification, bone-black is often mixed with them, and after remaining a month or two they are filtered through charcoal.

The chemical composition of fish oil is very complicated, as it contains volatile odors, acids, gall, and different salts. Fish oil is used as a burning fluid, for making soft soaps, and adulterating other oils, and by the manufacturers of chamois leather.

Sperm Oil and Spermaceti

In the head and special cavities of the cranium of several Cetacei, especially of the pot-fish or cachalot, and some species of dolphins, there is a liquid fat from which, after the death of the animal, a large quantity of a white, firm, tallow-like substance is separated.

The liquid part is what is called sperm oil, and the solid part spermaceti.

The sperm oil is found in commerce bleached and unbleached, the latter having a brownish appearance and disagreeable odor; chemically regarded, it is very interesting. It is easily saponified and the soap resulting is readily solved in water. The spermaceti is almost exclusively used for luxus candles.

Oleic Acid

Though no animal fat, but occurring from such, we will say a few words on it in addition to the above-described fats. Oleic acid or red oil is a product incidental to the manufacture of adamantine candles.

There are two kinds in commerce. The one formed by the process of distillation is only fit for making soft soap, owing to its disagreeable odor, whilst the other, the result of simple pressure, yields soaps of great consistency, whether saponified alone or with an admixture of tallow or other fats.

In cool weather, oleic acid has a mushy consistency, attributable to the solidification of the solid fat which it reduces from the stearine cakes, and amounts to ten or fifteen percent It often contains a small amount of sulphuric acid, hence, it should be borne in mind, that oleic acid ought to be washed with some weak lye before using it.

It is not only employed by soap makers, but also by other manufacturers, and is therefore an article very much in demand.

Elaidic Acid

By the action of hyponitric acid upon oleic acid, a pearly white, crystalline substance is obtained, of the consistence of tallow, and termed elaidic acid. It is manufactured on a large scale in England, since-it has been found that it is equally serviceable to both soap and candle manufacturers.

Chapter 5- Soap Recipes

Windsor Soap

1. (White.) The best "English Windsor Soap" is made of a mixture of

Olive oil 1 part,

Ox suet, or tallow 8 or 9 parts

Saponified with lye of caustic soda, and scented after removal from the boiler.

The ordinary, in general, is merely curd-soap, scented, whilst semi-liquid, with oil of caraway, supported with a little oil of bergamot, lavender, or origanum.

To the finer qualities a very little oil of cassia, or of almonds, or of the essences of musk and ambergris, is also commonly added. The usual proportion of the mixed oils for good qualities, is 1 1/2 lbs. per cwt., and 2 lbs., at the least, for the finer ones, exclusive of the alcoholic essences, if any be employed. The fatty basis of "French Windsor Soap" is usually hog's lard, with the addition of a little palm oil.

2. (Brown.) Originally this was the white variety that had become yellow and brown by age. It now merely differs from the preceding in being colored with a little caramel, or (less frequently), with umber or brown ochre.

Honey Soap

The ordinary "honey soap" is merely the finest bright-colored yellow (resin) soap, colored by the addition of a little palm oil or palm oil soap, and scented with oil of rose geranium, or oil of gingergrass, supported or not with a little oil of bergamot or verbena.

Some of the finer kinds are made of

Olive oil soap 1 part

Palm oil soap 1 part

White curd soap 3 parts

deepened in color, whilst in the liquid state, with a little palm oil, or annotto (of its tincture), and scented with 1 to 11 ounces of essential oils per 1/2 lb., or 1 to 11/2 lbs. per cwt.

Musk Soap

The basis is generally a good ox suet or tallow soap; the scent, essence of musk, or oil of musk, supported with a little of the oils of bergamot, cinnamon, and cloves.

The quantity of the essence used depends on the intended quality (fragrance) of the product.

The coloring matter is usually caramel. This soap, when sufficiently scented, imparts a faint but persistent odor to the skin, which is very agreeable. "Ambergris soap" is prepared in a similar way.

Glycerinated Soap

Any mild toilet soap, with which about – 1/25th to 1/20th of its weight of glycerine has been intimately incorporated whilst in the liquid state.

It is generally tinged of a red or rose color, or orange-yellow. It is variously scented; but oil of bergamot, or rose geranium (ginger-grass), supported with a little oil of cassia, or cassia supported with essential oil of almonds, appear to be its favorite perfumes.

We are obliged to Struve, proprietor of a large soap factory in Leipsic (Germany), for the following receipt for glycerinated soap:

40 lbs. of tallow, 40 lbs. of lard, and 20 lbs. of cochin coconut oil, are saponified with 45 lbs. of soda lye and 5 lbs. of potash lye of 40 Baume, when the soap is to be made in the cold way.

To the paste are then added

Pure glycerine 6 lbs.

Oil of Portugal ½ ounce.

Oil of bergamnot ½ ounce.

Bitter almond oil 5 ounces.

Oil of vitivert 3 ounces.

Almond Soap

The best quality is usually white curd soap, with or without the addition of 1/9th to 1/7th of its weight of olive oil soap, scented with essential oil of almonds in the proportion of about 1 ounce to each 41/2 to 5 lbs., or 11/2 lbs. to the cwt; very fine.

The addition of a little oil of cassia (say 4 or 5 ounces per cwt), improves it. Second and inferior qualities are scented with nitrobenzole, the artificial oil of almonds, instead of the genuine or natural oil.

Violet Soap

1. Any white toilet soap strongly scented with essence of orris root, and colored, or not, with tincture of litmus, or a little levigated smalts, ultramarine, or indigo.

2. White curd soap 3 lbs.,

Olive oil soap 1 lb.,

Palm oil soap 3 lbs.,

melted together, and further scented (best cold) with a little essence of orris root, and colored, or not, at will. Very fragrant, but it does not take color very well.

Bouquet Soap

1. Take of---

White curd soap, finest. 17 ½ lbs.,

Olive oil soap 2 ½ lbs.,

Oil of bergamot 1 ounce,

Cassia 1 ½ drachms

Cloves 1 ½ drachms

Sassafras 1 ½ drachms

Thyme 1 ½ drachms

Neroli 1 drachm,

Ochre, brown, levigated 2 ounces,

and proceed as for almond soap. Highly and agreeably fragrant. It may be varied by substituting English oil of lavender for the "neroli."

2. Take of---

White curd soap. 20 lbs.

Oil of bergamot 2 2/3 ounces. "

Cloves ½ drachm

Neroli ½ drachm

Sassafras 1/3 drachm

Thyme 1/3 drachm

Colored with 2 1/2 ounces brown ochre.

Lavender Soap

The basis of the "Windsor soap," scented with English oil of lavender (1 to 1 1/2 fluid ounces per 7 lbs.), supported with a little oil of bergamot and the essences of musk and ambergris. It is often colored with a little tincture of litmus, or the corresponding mineral pigments.

Orange Flower Soap

As " savon a la rose;" but using pure neroli, supported with a "dash' of the essences of ambergris and Portugal, instead of otto of roses, as scent. A delicate yellow tinge is sometimes given to it. The French soap, " A la fleur d'orange," is scented with equal parts of neroli and geranium.

About The Author

Geraldine McDaniel learned the art of basic soap making from her grandmother and then went on to learn a whole lot more about the soap making process as she was interested in making it a business to support herself and her family.

With the right set of tools in hand and the support of her family she started to make soap and sell them to the stores in her town. She also has quite a thriving online business as well. Her book helps other to learn just what it takes to make good soap.

Lightning Source UK Ltd.
Milton Keynes UK
UKHW02f1851031018
329963UK00016B/565/P

9 781632 874719